*Coffee is for*

*Closers*

...

Created and published by Shelley Renee
Breatheandreboot.com
© 2019 Shelley Renee
All rights reserved

No part of this product may be used or reproduced in any manner whatsoever without prior written permission from the publisher.

*Write on!*

www.ingramcontent.com/pod-product-compliance
Lightning Source LLC
Chambersburg PA
CBHW030646220526
45463CB00005B/1662